GW00393937

A FOUNTAIN STIRRED

POETRY

BY

BRIAN G. DAVIES

The Wolfian Press

"Waiting"

Every day you do not come
A little bit of summer dies...."

Helen Holland

IN MEMORIAM

This collection of poems is dedicated to Maureen, my wife for almost 47 years, and the love of my life. She was cruelly snatched from us earlier this year, succumbing very quickly to an aggressive cancer of the pancreas. She was honest, hardworking and straightforward, and fiercely loyal to friends and family. Only 73, she had many more fulfilling years ahead of her, and had hoped to see her three grandchildren come of age. Maureen displayed a deep-seated faith in God, and was loved and respected by all who knew her. Her passing into Glory leaves a big hole in the lives of all who knew her.

October 2014

"My mind is troubled, like a fountain stirred,
and I myself see not the bottom of it"

Troilus & Cressida

AUTHOR'S BIOGRAPHY

Born in 1933 in South London of Welsh parentage , Brian was at the start of World War Two one of London's evacuees. Having spent a year as such in a small South Wales mining village he was then sent as a boarder to King's School, Ely in Cambridgeshire, where he remained until the war's end. Returning home in 1945, Brian transferred to Alleyn's College, Dulwich, and in 1952 was called up for National Service, initially at the Tower of London, but eventually joining the R.A.E.C. Most of this period was served as an educational Sergeant Instructor in Singapore.

Following his demob, Brian spent three years studying to qualify as a teacher. After some years as such in various schools he withdrew from the teaching profession and turned instead to commerce as a management consultant, working for various "blue-chip" companies. During this period he met Maureen, his wife-to-be, also a teacher, and they had two children. Over a considerable period they owned several motorhomes and spent many holidays travelling throughout the U.K. and on the continent. This enabled them to indulge their passion for exploration and travel while broadening the experiences of their children. Amongst their travels they followed the Pilgrim Route to Compostela, and ascended several of France's highest passes.

Brian is now retired and lives in a small market town in the Welsh Marches, where he is organist for a near-by Methodist chapel. Both he and Maureen were widely-travelled, enjoyed reading, music, gardening, and the company of their three young grandchildren, currently living in South Wales. Brian also writes travel articles and poems, several of which have been published in various magazines.

The PANCREATIC CANCER RESEARCH FUND

Pancreatic cancer is the deadliest disease of its kind. It is aggressive and unrelenting, and has the lowest survival rate of all cancers. Of the more than 8 thousand people diagnosed annually, just 3% survive for longer than five years. Research has been both limited and under-funded, and it is the only cancer which has seen little or no improvement in its long-term survival rate for over 40 years.

Relatively few people have heard of, or come across, cancer of the pancreas. Chances are most do not know where this organ is located or what it does, even though it plays a major part in the body's metabolism and digestive system. Around 6 inches long, it lies behind the stomach and is adjacent to the liver. Initial diagnosis can be difficult as symptoms are often only noticeable in its later stages, by which time it is usually impossible to treat. Major signals can be back, shoulder and stomach pain, indigestion, weight loss and even jaundice. GPs may confuse these with problems like ulcers, gastritis or even other cancers, and treatments can be limited to tablets in an attempt to mask the resultant pains. Delay in diagnosis, coupled with inappropriate treatment, soon allows the cancer to spread to the liver and into the bones, by which stage (Stage 4, terminal) is arrived at.

More research therefore is sorely needed into both the causes and diagnosis of pancreatic cancer, and its possible treatment. Every day 22 people are diagnosed with this silent but most aggressive of diseases.It is the fifth most common cause of all cancer deaths and, despite its high death rate, it attracts very little funding for research, less than 2% of all such funding annually. Maggie Blanks is founder of the charity (PCRF), having established it some twelve years ago following the death of her husband from the disease. She had been shocked to discover that there was no dedicated source of finance, and says that the charity's mission is to attract funding and to allocate it in order to promote innovate research which will lead to a more effective detection and treatment of this most destructive of cancers.

Profits from the sales of this book of poetry, conceived in memory of my wife Maureen, who passed away from the disease in April 2014 after a short illness, will be donated to the Pancreatic Cancer Research Fund.

<u>INDEX</u>

For Children

Elephant It Is
Elephanting
Cause For Fear
Absence Makes the Heart
Little Helpers
Pretend

THE DEPARTING AGE

Away my youth is flowing, fast as the ebbing tide
Towards the endless void of black eternity.
As swift as lightning flashing through the sky.
Darting through crowded space; its aim, its goal,
To extinguish life upon this teeming sphere.
Life, unappreciated, on its flight
To Heaven speeds, as looks an angel lost
With yearning eyes and upstretched arms to God
When sunk in the infernal black morass.

Lost irrevocably is all that's past;
The flame of youth now wavers, wanes and fades.
But one last moment yet the dying embers
Enjoy their glorious being,
Burning brighter than ever,
Only to cease with startling suddenness,
Leaving their owner's gaze firm fixed upon
The dull and frigid ash of Middle Age.

UNKNOWN DESTINY

Free, and yet not free, the ties of school are broken,
No longer are we tethered to our mother's apron-strings.
The binding shackles shatter, the way to fame lies open,
The road is strewn with flowers, the choice is freely ours,
To trudge along the rut, or to climb with outstretched wings.

And yet, there is the rub; ahead of us, unending
There gapes the black abyss, with unknown dangers fraught.
The higher we ascend, the quicker we, descending,
Meet with our peril great, the road is not so straight,
And advancing into line we face the troubles war has brought.

WAR; it stills our breath, our beating hearts are quiet.
We await the great awakening when, free from worldly strife,
Our earthly bodies still, while our souls run riot,
A force without an aim, the method still the same,
A forward flanking movement, the prize Eternal Life.

From among those souls competing, which shall attain the prize?
Which shall be doomed for ever, and which have grace to live?
The thoughts of those departed come into those which rise
But, until we hear the call, put our backs against the wall
And defend the Blessed Peace which the Lord is pleased to give.

THE TRANSFORMING TOUCH

As night succeeds the dawn,
So silently ephemeral Beauty leaves familiar haunts,
To pass along Time's travel-weary way,
Preferring not to cast a glance behind
And so the passing shades of life regret.
But rather to press on to bear Oblivion's vilest taunts
And face its bitter scorn.

Yet Beauty must not die;
Her former glories ravaged by the coarsened hand of Time.
The vital life-blood of her very soul
Set idly flowing by an anxious Fate.
She must not die, for in this transient life
The death of gentle Beauty is too terrible a crime
To light Man's progress by.

Eternity is long.
It stretches from beginnings born before the light of day
Illumined Earth; there is no end to it.
So Man must sink into the dust of time –
No flower can become a bud again.
And Beauty too eventually must fade and pass away,
An echo of Life's song.

What matters then her death?
For even brief existence lights the shadowed path of Man.
The breeze a ripple on the water lays.
So rather, Beauty in the mem'ry lives
And in its working-out be more aware
Than in her very being. Now is seen thus only can
She draw eternal breath.

So shall Man's beauty live.
Though beauty of the body is indeed a mortal flower
Which strives without success Time to restrain.
That beauty blossoming in the soul of Man
Indeed possesses an Eternity.
Yet would that Man could to his actions hour by hour
A touch of Beauty give.

LANDSCAPE OF LIFE

Like the vine they cling,
Seeking to gain their strength from the support
Of sturdy poles.
Seeking to raise themselves towards the sun
Which beams above.
And in its rays
They go their careless way,
Knowing no whys or wherefores, only sure
The world is theirs.

      Softly pass the years.
      There is no end to childhood; though today
      Is gone for good
      Tomorrow comes instead, but in its turn
      Is called Today.
      So sees a child the landscape of his life.
      His being is the present, for he knows
      The world is his.

      Wherefore comes that joy
      Which courses in our veins and leads us back
      Through childhood hours?
      For in the presence of a child is born
      The hope we may
      Put off Autumn's cloak, and gently take
      The tender, trusting hand of Spring and know
      The world is ours.

Linger while you may,
And grasp with eager hands the falling fruit
Of present joys.
Drink of the sparkling waters from the fount
Of transient youth.
Now stalks the spectre Time; his hand is soon
Upon your head. Not for much longer shall
The world be yours.

GOODBYE, MY FRIEND

Lowered into an earthy grave,
The blackness swallowing up what I had known
So short a time before, had claimed as friend.
This – now no more than putrefying clay
Devoid of beauty, thought…..
Deprived of life –
Condemned for ever to abhor the light,
To shelter rather in the arms of Death.
This – this had been you; that youthful face still seems
To haunt the careless dimness of the night,
Though reason tells me that this cannot be,
For I am here, alive, and you, my friend
Are passing from the cares of yesterday
Into the vacuum of Eternity.

Now, even as I look, the earth begins
To fall; at first, quite slowly, then with gathering pace.
The lighter grains are softly trickling in
To knock with timid touch upon that wall
Of wood encasing thy fragility.
You do not wake, nor even when the clods
Begin to fall and cover up from sight
All trace that you were born, have lived, have loved,
Have fought and wrestled, hated, laughed and cried.

Did you indeed exist, or were you but
A passing shadow on the field of Life?
I felt your hand upon my consciousness,
Your very being guiding on my way.
Your thoughts were mine, my warm desires were yours,
How real to me your presence ever was.
And yet, whene'er I in the mirror look
I closer come to knowing thee than e'er
I did when you were oft-times at my side.

Within that shrouded dwelling is interred
Far more than any seeking eye could see;
The shadow of a friendship free conferred
And, close beside my friend, lies - ME.

I SHALL NOT RETURN

No, I shall not return;
The warm and silent night
Will put the world to sleep
In the moon's enfolding light.

My body will not be there,
And through the latticed hole
A freshening breeze will steal,
Enquiring for my soul.

Will any await my return
Through long and weary years?
Or kiss my memory
Between their caresses and tears?

UNATTAINABLE

That which is now, shall fade and pass away;
All will be still, no sound shall stir the air.
Silence, that god, shall reign supreme around,
     All life shall cease, no movement anywhere.

That which was once, shall ne'er again disturb
The empty air, devoid of sense or sound;
No echo e'er again shall break apart
     The bonds of peace, which earth at last has found.

No more shall conquering armies march to war,
Hear the ground shake beneath the tramp of feet.
No more shall mingle joy and helpless terror,
     Hearken, ye Gods, where foe and victor meet.

Death, when it comes, in varying forms and manner,
Stealing this human soul away by night;
Wrong shall be conquered, enemy defeated,
     Emerge as victor the eternal right,

MAN IT IS

Where God went wrong
Was not to create Man in His own image,
Nor yet to clothe in transient flesh his soul.
Not even to give him a life eternal,
No, God went wrong at first when Man grew old.

Why God went wrong
Was not because Pandora's box was opened,
Was not because the serpent tempted Eve.
Nor yet because in Noah's flood He drowned him,
No, God went wrong in letting Man grow old.

When God went wrong
The angels cried aloud and hid their faces;
The birds and beasts and fishes fled in fear.
The heavens wept, the planets dimmed their lanterns;
When God went wrong 'twas only Man grew old.

That God went wrong
Is clear when blooming youths and maidens wither,
Is evidenced when boys and girls transmute
Through seven ages to their lonely dotage.
That God went wrong we know, for Man grows old.

So God went wrong,
And Man the consequences has to suffer.
His bones grow weak, his flesh corrupts and dies.
The beauty of his youth lasts but a moment,
For God went wrong, but Man it is grows old.

EXPECTATION

I lived for love, and life, and liberty;
I was as others are, happy and free.
No longer can I live, for darkness shackles me -
    I cannot see.

Surrounded, yet alone, I try to find
My tortuous way through life, a life that's lined
With fears of the unknown, but people still are kind -
    For I am blind.

I fear to face the future, for no light
Shines through the echoing darkness of my plight.
I cannot share the scenes that give you such delight -
    I have no sight.

I stumble through a world unknown to me.
I cannot be aware of flower or tree
Save by its smell or touch, I know not scenery –
    I want to see!

And yet – 'though through the darkness I must grope,
A void where lies the pitfall and the slope.
Perhaps will come the day when for myself I'll cope -
    I still have hope.

THE ROAD TO DESTINY

I walked along the road to Destiny,
Between tall palings of three-storied thoughts,
Minding not to place unheeding feet
Athwart the cracks between the tombston'd plans
Of those who earlier had walked this way.
Side-stepped the battered rubbish of their rusted hopes
And, careful not to tread the refuse of their lust,
Kept my gaze fixed firmly on the mem'ry of the past.

A grass-green park approached and beckoned me
To pass between its portals of despair.
Careful to avoid their leprous touch
I cautiously drew near the mirror'd plane,
A silver slab set in an emerald dream.
I gazed, and the reflection showed me what I feared –
Where once we played as children our past is lying drowned
And as I look again I see ourselves within her arms.

I walked once more beneath the thund'rous sky
Of dead desires and unfulfilled intents.
Along the dim-lit corridor of truth
The shrouded mammals blindly pushed their way;
Their words like pellets showering from their lips,
Each word a book of nonsense never to be read.
And from the gaping windows of their transient minds
Streamed out the light of nothingness to join the passing void.

Another pocket-handkerchief of green
Impinged upon my sight, but this time Death
Had stamped his fiery claw on those who rest
Within their shaded box. Their souls cried out
In vain attempts to fasten on my life.
If this is where life leads, then all indeed is vain
And mem'ry but a shadow of our former selves,
Tramping the ethereal air, impermanent and null.

THE TURNING OF THE WORM

What did you see out there?
A shape, a shadow or a ghostly wraith?
A fleeting glimpse of Promise? Did you dare
To venture forth and claim a friend in faith?

I left the narrow safety of my way;
Stretched forth my hand to hold
The Promise glittering in the light of day -
But found it was not gold.

What do you see out there?
Now that the worm is turned, is seen to be
A creature bent and bitter? Do you care
That from what once had snared you, you are free?

When men begin to query why their friends
Profess their friends to be,
The shallow roots dry up, the friendship ends,
The canker kills the tree.

What will you see out there?
There was no substance in that passing cloud.
Much as the bait within the mousetraps snare
Their victims, did not this nimbus prove a shroud?

What is this man who wastes another's gift?
How can he know its cost?
How can he face the next that fate shall lift?
Before he starts - he's lost.

THIS SOUND OF LOVE

I remember - What?

What was that sound that just now touched
My straining ears
And then in silence slipped away?
     The sound as of a glittering waterfall
     Cascading o'er the rocky precipice
     And so crescendoing its turbulent passage
     To the stormy ocean.
And yet it was the sound of singing too;
The rising and falling of a multitude
Of treble voices singing endless praises
To a glorious Godhead.
     But no; perhaps it was more like the sound
     Made by the all-pervading wind which seeks
     To range from highest mountain-top to lowest furrow
     Kissing all creation.

Once more that sound returns to lie
Within my heart
Before it softly steals away.
     A sound as of the swinging of the lamp
     Which lights the weary traveller to the door
     Where, safe behind that stout, unyielding portal,
     He finds at last his rest.
And yet, it seemed it was the sound which Heaven
Has planted in the beauty of Man's youth,
'Though which, as hoary Time his way approaches,
Increasingly recedes.
     But no, perhaps this time it more resembles
     The trembling passage of a lover's glance
     Which, crashing through the air, binds fast the loved one
     With silv'ry chords of love.

And, as the silence slips away,
My straining ears
Again recall this sound of love.

I remember - Now.

PASSING MOMENT

It has gone, slipped through my clutching fingers
Like sparkling waters sliding softly on;
Alone, in arid space, the vibrant mem'ry lingers,
But the moment of our love has gone.

Could I conjure up thine arrowed glances
Or e'en thy fleeting spoken words recall?
This memory of thee the present hour enhances;
Bitter was that moment of my fall.

Fast within my arms lay that perfection
Which I had sought, and only lately gained.
Sweet is this deep-drunk draught of mazy recollection,
Sorrowful that moment Love was stained.

Is love nothing but a brief sensation
Which for a moment pauses, then moves on?
Yet am I folded close in mindful contemplation;
Love is present still, though thou art gone.

Think not that thy gift now lies unheeded;
The breeze a ripple on the water lays.
So shall I love thee when this present has receded,
Deep embosomed in Time's misty greys.

So shall I love thee, when all else widely scatters;
Of Love, and Love's frail moment, only its being matters.

VIETNAM REMEMBERED
(inspired by the Vietnam War)

It is dawning…..
The sun begins its weary climb into the
Wakening sky.
The chatter of the creatures far below disturbs
The quiet
Of their jungle home. The turgid river
Slyly slinks
Along its broadening path; the rotting
Vegetation stinks –
And it is morning.

> A man is stirring.
> Soon will these pulsing jungle glades re-echo
> To the sound
> Of human voices. Soon will be awake
> Those other
> Women, men and children who,
> In spite of eastern strife,
> Spurn what they are shown, reject
> The western way of life –
> Their own preferring.

The silence shatters
As, borne on silvery wings the angry hornet
Buzzes nearer,
Its sting prepared to inject a helpless
Population.
The cloud draws on, its shadow over
Green-flecked landscape races,
And even when towards it turn those
Apprehensive faces –
It hardly matters.

The rain is falling.
A gentle and beguiling rain which soothes those
Troubled hearts.
And silences for ever minds which rashly
Dare to challenge.
The rain of rockets, napalm bombs, flash
To that jungle clearing;
The cotton-wool of phosphorus
Prevents the raiders hearing
Those voices calling.

This confrontation
Of tender flesh and burning metal turn the
Gentle breezes
Of the humid jungle into a raging wild
Inferno.
Flesh shrivels up, the sickly stench
Pervades the man-made night.
And still the metal vultures circle,
Wondering at this sight
Of desolation.

A child lies crying.
Its bloody, mangled arm outstretched in muted
Supplication.
A babe, torn from its mother's breast, lies broken
In the ruins
Of what was once its home. Amidst this
War of escalation
No antiseptic miracle, nor
Urgent operation
Can save their dying.

It is evening ………
With pain-attended effort the bomb-burned victims
Reach their end.
Their journey done, they pass on leaving War and
Hate behind.
But still the fractious nations fight
With weapon and with word
And 'midst this noise the victims cannot –
Nay, will not - be heard,
For ever grieving.

THE RETURN

He turns, he pants, he turns again and once more stumbles on,
Eyes straining to the distance, yet unseeing.
The blood pounds in his ears,
His heart is beating a fast tattoo upon his ribs,
But all he hears is the plod, plod of his feet against the earth,
Stone-hard, unyielding as he stumbles, stumbles, falls,
Picks himself up and stumbles on again.

He stops, again he turns and strains to catch the distant sounds,
But only hears the pounding in his chest.
The scene before his eyes
Says all is peaceful, though the evidence is there.
His mind rejects the atmosphere of calm, for tumult reigns
Inside himself – a chaos more primeval than
The slime and slough from which life first emerged.

He turns again, once more to push his weary flesh along
The track he's followed since that day began
To stain the sky with tears.
The streaks had spread, at last the cloak of darkness fell
Away, to show the waking world this parody of Man,
A soul in torment fleeing from its captors, who
Relentlessly pursue the fugitive.

Too late! His mist-dimmed eyes have failed to give him warning,
And his ears, blocked by the thunderous sounds within,
Have left their work undone.
An arm approaches, rises to his shoulder, lays an iron hand
Which now grips, grips, to prevent an incautious move.
The cuffs click fast, the key is turned, and all prepare
To return the errant prisoner to his cell.

EXODUS

That which we know not of,
How shall we ever learn?
We leave that peaceful haven where our hearts did burn
With childish pride,
Where once we did enjoy
The fellowship and company so dear to many a boy.
Where, sheltered from the world,
We led a sheltered life
Far from the blood and tears of the eternal strife.

How shall we face it?
Shall we turn and run,
Or shall we show the others how it should be done?
That we can face undaunted
All that at us is hurled.
That we can raise our banners and, with flag unfurled,
Stand firm, as should a warrior
Who battles for the right.
And prove to them that learning is stronger far than might.

Our schooldays were not wasted,
For we have learned to face
The rushing world with eagerness,
And in it take our place.

A PEAK OF LAND

Why is it that I choose to climb so high?
 Is it to escape the dubious pleasures of the plain,
Or flee the fickle camaraderie of my fellow-man?
Atop this peak of land I choose to stand,
Enjoy the pleasant company of fowl and flower;
To feel beneath my foot the reassuring strength
Of igneous rock, to catch the gleam of quartz
Amongst the lichen, hear the early bubbling
Of an infant river, e'er to its destiny it strays.

Far below, as soldiers on a map group and re-group for war,
Inhabitants of village or of farm play out their time,
Partake the daily routine of their ways,
Passing from love to hatred, joy to fear, all in an instant
Of eternity. But I, atop this peak of land whereon I stand
Am aeons away from artificial aid and empty ends.
I savour morning mist and following sunshine, evening light
Breaking across the woolly ramparts of the clouding sky
To flood the wondering rivers of my mind with ruby rays.

So darkness falls, the shadows lengthen, creep across the valley floor,
Ascending rocky slopes far faster than my feet did earlier climb.
Time to descend, to mix again with life at lower levels
Where flows afresh the tyrant tide of time, be swept along
The rocky gorge of humdrum daily living, be cast at last
Upon the veiled shores of after-life.
Why not remain, atop this peak of land where I still stand?
Descent is now imperilled by the darkness, cold the hand
Of him who walks beside along that path.

   Remain and rest, await that glorious dawning which, so soon
   Will set you free from earthly trammel, set you on the path
   To other glories, whilst your frame for ever rests
   In splendid solitude atop that peak of land where lately you did stand.

THE THIEF

If, in the gathering darkness, someone call,
An echo of the past is conjured forth
To wreak upon my quivering memory-chord
A havoc which, unpitying as a whore,
Steals all of value from my naked frame
    And leaves me but my name.

Once, lonely as a rock upon a shore,
I stood unwashed by any tide of warmth.
The force of love had yet to breach the wall
Within the shade of which my life was moored.
And then I saw that love was mine to give
    And I began to live.

What purpose lay within the deepness of my mind?
What reason brought I to the whirlpool of desire?
I caught at sunbeams, but each golden ray defined
Was tainted by the flame of an unbridled fire.

And now my love lies shattered on the floor,
With mocking, scornful glance she let it fall.
There now remains no trace within the store-house
Of my heart of that which once was worth
A treasure greater than all earth could boast,
    'Though searched from coast to coast.

So, if in gathering darkness, someone call,
Unfettered passion from my breast is poured.
In turbulent, fiery streams it flows once more
As mem'ry to the past again gives birth.
And as these treasures from the past I steal,
    My lover's touch I feel.

<u>WITHIN..........WITHOUT</u>

Within these walls we live and pass our days,
  Until that hour when we may up and go
Out to the world once more, into that maze
  Which is called Life – and join its futile ebb and flow.

Within these walls there is no beauty found
  But what is sown and tended in the mind
Of every man, to whom the daily round
  Is the antithesis of what is left behind.

For Beauty, Truth and Honour dormant lie,
  And through each man's existence hourly crawls
The slime of his dishonour, whilst his cry,
  Shorn of all hope, reverberates around these walls.

Though time drags by our thoughts fly on apace.
  The wall is but the epicycle of all
Who look to seeing once again in grace
  That Beauty, Honour, Truth flourish without the wall.

PALEST FIRE

Soft thy glances, little one;
Jealously I watch thee.
With discerning eyes caress the contours of thy face.
Long each moment to appraise
That vital, youth-born glory,
Striking palest fire from thy beautifying grace.

Soft thy smile, my little one,
Hungrily I taste thee.
Breathe in close communion the fragrance of thy love.
Fasten on thine upturned face
Devouring lips in search of
Lasting joy and beauty – can nectar sweeter prove?

Soft thine answer, little one;
Desperately I want thee.
Letting fall from fresh-loved lips those words which beckon on.
Turn not from exquisite pathways
Where love's joy treads strongly,
Or what shall remain to me when thou, my love, art gone?

So –
Soft thy touch, my little one,
Tenderly I take thee.
Fold about thy quickened form Love's gentle winding-sheet.
Soft this softest contact
Heralding the blush of morning.
Comes anew this love to us e'er wrapt in Death's deceit.

AWAKENING

As though from far away
   Insidious whispers seek to undermine the wall
   Of my defences;
Whilst hazy glimpses of exquisite joy strip all
   Of my pretences
And show them to be clay.

For it was not to be
   That ancient mists would veil for ever the desire
   And expectation
Which did in fever'd youth burn brightly and inspire
   This sweet temptation
And now again I see.

And bravely though I try
   To stem the tide which steals unseen upon the shore
   Of my decision,
It is in vain; I weep at Fate's sardonic caw
   Of harsh derision.
My resolutions die.

Yet can we ever know
   The anguished torments of the mind which starts
   Insanely burning?
Can any understand the thoughts which set a heart
   Profanely yearning
To reap what lovers sow?

What passions come to view
   As now once-gentle rivers scour their cleansing way
   To unseen oceans.
Obscurant mists of doubt pass on and so display
   Erotic motions
Which to their end pursue.

GRAVE MEMORIES

Every day, I said, that I would visit you.
    Put fresh flowers on your lonely grave,
Though all about are others who have passed this way.
Their loved ones put mementos at the head of those held dear.
They come each day, each week, they come perhaps each year
    To clear old flowers, cut the grass, set up again
Mementos which have fallen, or been blown.

Your life was more than this, and even fragrant flowers
    Cannot replace that which I now do miss.
Your smile, your touch, your warmth, your love – all gone now
And in the cold rememberance of every breaking day
Memories of us together crowd in from every side.
    In places where I visit, I am now aware
Of something, someone, who perhaps is you.

A softling sound, a sigh, will reinforce your absence,
    A fleeting glance will bring you back to mind.
Here in my heart is room enough, as ever was,
For you who shared my life, was always here or near.
So stay with me, my sweetling; even though the flowers
    No longer have a scent, nor hold their fragrant smell,
Their colours still enliven these dark days.

Necessity converted flowers into silks.
    Silks do not fade nor wither; whilst they stay
They are an outward symbol of an inward love
As are those likenesses in photo album or on wall.
Your mem'ry will not wither whilst my breath I draw.
    So sleep within your wooden cradle 'neath my feet
Until once more you wake, and together we shall be.

CENTRE OF MY UNIVERSE

The glimmering stars are falling from the blackly-painted
firmament
    of night;
The mystic heavens have opened wide their casements, from which
stream in
    endless flight
Those lanterns serving still to light the pathway of a wandering
soul
    in space,
And guide that spirit which, not moments past, had fled the features
    of thy face,
And left it without trace,
Embalmed in deathly white.

Athwart the dark-drest messenger of Hades soaring rampant
through
    the skies
Thy spirit claws reluctantly its path across the rainbow
    of my sighs.
I hold within my firm-fixed arms the shadow of thy death-
encompassed
    frame,
The substance sadly struck, a moment past, from this dear shell;
    is this a game?
I softly call thy name;
With thee the echo dies.

Those eyes which into mine so often gazed, and with their beauty
 held me fast,
Are now by heavy-lidded death enchained, my sweetling hours
with thee
 are past.
Thy tender, silk-smooth limbs upon the counterpane of Life
 so coldly lie.
No longer will thy warming touch arouse within my breaking heart
 a cry.
But our love cannot die,
Though you're asleep at last.

Soon shall the chasm open at my feet, thy wood-swathed temple
 to receive,
And I of that sweet centre of my universe reluctant
 take my leave.
A toneless chanting moans about my ears as heavily
 I turn away,
Now bearing but the mem'ry of a dream to light the shadows
 of the day
My darling turned to clay,
And I was left to grieve.

MY LIGHT, MY WORLD

You are missed so much,
Your laughter, sense of fun.
Since first we met, you were the only one.
So kind, so helpful,
Always there for me.
Watching out for pitfalls
Wherever they might be.

You held my hand
And guided me through life.
'Twas the best day
When you became my wife.
We had our work, our children came -- and went!
They have their own lives now,
Although yours is spent.

It was too soon,
Our lives had long to run.
You, always mine, you were my light, my sun.
We were together
Throughout each night and day.
Faced up to any trouble
In our special way.

But, when Death came calling
For that angel in my life
There was nothing could be done
To save my darling wife.
So, alone and lonely, what is there now to do
But pass the love of both of us
Onto our children too.

You were loved so much;
Now, you are missed so much.......

JESUS IS LISTENING

Jesus is listening, loving us
As with a shepherd's care;
Guiding his flock from sinful ways,
Teaching the power of prayer.
Jesus is listening, will he hear
Voices to Heaven raised?
His arms enfold as we draw near,
His glorious name be praised.

Jesus is waiting, come to Him,
No longer turn away.
Nothing the world can offer you
Is worthy of delay.
Jesus is waiting to bestow
Salvation on each one;
Who follows Christ His love will know,
His heavenly will be done.

Jesus is asking for my word
That I will follow Him.
I'll march triumphant with my Lord
When this world's glories dim.
Jesus is asking – shall I say
Take me and make me Thine?
Thy cleansing blood brings love and hope
And perfect peace divine.

Jesus is coming, me to save,
He died at Calvary.
And when at last He comes again
I know He'll come for me.
Jesus is coming, wave the palms,
It was for me He died.
And when He takes me in His arms
I shall be purified.

Jesus has listened, did I say
He is my everything?
I'll wait no longer for that day,
My life to Him I'll bring.
Jesus is now my resting-place,
No longer will I roam.
So, as I march towards my Lord
I know I'm coming home.

MY ONE AND ONLY

Could I ever think to love another?
    I have loved sister, father, aunt and mother.
    Even loved my cat, my dog, my brother,
But more than all together was my love for you.

Many years ago I dwelt at home,
    But then came the impulse to be gone.
    Leaving all behind I was to roam
Until that day encountering my signing-post.

Can you hear the ringing of the church bell?
    It's sending out the message of your death-knell.
    I can feel your presence that I knew well
And cherished day by day whilst you stood by my side.

My memory's short, but memories are long.
    Life's for living, breathing, with each song
    Bringing each day forward, pushing strong,
'Til we exist together in our brave new world.

So as I walk towards my final years
    And in the porch of Life confront my fears.
    I speak with her, and wonder that she hears,
For I am here, above, whilst she's below, at rest.

PEBBLES ON A BEACH

Standing at the cliff's edge, I remember well the day
That we stood here together, before you went away.
    The breeze was blowing gently, the sun it shone so bright
    For troubles were behind us, and everything seemed right.
    Our lives still stretched before us - we did not ask for more –
    But Time was fast encroaching, like the waves upon the shore.
The rocks would soon the pebbles make, and then would come to sand
But we knew nought of worry as we stood there, hand in hand.

The breeze is getting stronger as day turns into night.
The sun is disappearing, its warmth now only slight.
    I hear the pebbles on the beach, the waves are strongly breaking;
    Against the promenade they crash, I hear the noise they're making.
    Now, back upon that cliff-top, I look ahead and sigh
    Wondering with broken heart why it was your turn to die.
Can I exist without you? I but await that day
When we shall join together, and at my side you'll lay.

So, now the days are dragging on, the nights are slipping by,
I cannot seem to fill the time without a tear-stained eye.
    At times I ask my God, and yours, but seem to get no answer
    To why of all the people here it was you struck down with cancer.
    You were the only one for me, and I, I know, for you,
    Overcoming everything, our love was strong and true.
But then, like pebbles on a beach, we moved at waves' behest
And still I stand here, waiting, whilst you are now at rest.

THE FINAL KISS

To see those lips that kissed you,
Those eyes that lately gazed into your own.
To touch those hands that once caressed you,
Those arms which once, when living, did embrace you.
To gaze upon that form, silent and still,
That body where once beat a living heart,
          Throbbing...........Pulsating

That body which in life, when held against you,
Sent hot blood coursing through your veins,
Stirring emotions -
Emotions once again as dormant as a crocus bulb
        In mid-December.

When will your life again be introduced to rapture?
Will soft caressing arms and upturned mouth ever again
Move you to that point of ecstasy just lately felt?
That interchange of breath 'tween love and lovers;
Whose lips are now as newly-chiselled marble,
        Meaning nothing.

They have been kissed by Death.

THE COUNTLESS DEAD

Can you imagine those marching off to war?
Numberless men who, whether rich or poor,
Whether, from shops or factories or farms,
Or squires' sons, all heeding the clarion call to arms.
Some saw it as their duty
To go and bash the Hun.
Whilst others left Life's drudgery
And thought it would be fun
To wear a smart new uniform, a rifle by their side,
And so across the Channel they travelled, fought and died.

The war would soon be over, and they'd be home again.
"See you all at Christmas" was the popular refrain.
But Christmas came, and Christmas went, and soon it was New
Year,
And trenches were those soldiers' homes, the end was still unclear.
Back home were wives and mothers,
Daughters, sweethearts, sons
But all around, by day or night
Was the thunder of the guns.
Houses were all flattened, and mud became the bed
Of countless volunteers, of whom were countless dead.

So day by day, and year by year the battle lines were drawn
And armies which stood face to face were mostly dead by dawn.
Artillery was now the king, from out a clear blue sky
Or dropping through the cloud and rain, it was a day to die.
It could be now, or later
They could be blown to bits.
And in every stinking crater
A stinking soldier sits.
Barbed wire was many a soldiers' shroud, on naught could they
depend
To come and free them, give them aid, an ignominious end.

Grenades, machine guns, then the gas, and after these came tanks.
Death was now the soldiers' friend, to wait for and give thanks.
Is there no hope for those who fight with bayonet and with gun?
The outcome may be capture, unless you cut and run.
Desertion was an option,
Recapture almost certain.
To be shot by one's own comrades
Would be the final curtain.
Some day our victory will come, with memories of this,
So keep your head down, soldier boy, and hope their bullets miss.

(Inspired by the Great War 1914-18)

FOR CHILDREN

ELEPHANT IT IS

I had a little elephant, I kept her in a shed,
And when she grew quite hungry I'd throw a loaf of bread.
I also gave her hay to eat, and a great big bowl of milk
Which, I know's, ambrosia to creatures of that ilk.

One morning when I went, I saw that she'd unlatched the door
And my little 'ellie wasn't with me any more.
She was a clever little thing and she had used her trunk,
Then stepped into the garden and quickly done a bunk.

She wandered down the High Street and tried to board a bus
But, size for size, she didn't fit, and caused an awful fuss.
She'd then gone down the station, and booked to Elmers End
For there it was my 'ellie hoped that she might find a friend.

The passengers were hopping mad as she took up twenty places,
But all went strangely quiet when she stared into their faces.
At journey's end the turnstiles wouldn't let her out the door
So my 'ellie used her weight and crushed them to the floor.

The stationmaster told her he'd had enough of hassle,
Advising her to take a train to the Elephant & Castle.
By the time she'd got there, it was growing dark
So a nice policeman directed her to Regent's Park.

Ellie asked a passing pigeon if what she'd heard was true,
That animals of every kind were welcomed at the Zoo.
Of course, the bird replied, the people there don't mind,
Even funny ones, like you, with tails in front and tails behind.

ELEPHANTING

Elephants are friendly,
They like bananas too,
As you would very clearly see
If you went to the zoo.
They have a super memory,
So if you make a date,
They're never never, hardly ever
Going to be late.

Elephants are curious
They want to know what's what,
They love to play in water
And then squirt the blinking lot.
They'd make an awful trumpeting
If you took away their bun
And chasing you around the zoo.
Would be their funny sense of fun

Elephants are helpful
And can carry lots of stuff.
They have to use their trunks of course,
But funnily enough,
Unlike the trunks you have at home
Theirs doesn't have a lid.
You can't pack anything inside;
You'd annoy him if you did.

So if you meet an elephant
Be cheerful and polite,
That elephant would want to know
That you would treat it right.
But if you try to take it home
It would very likely say
"I'm sorry little boy (or girl)
But I live the other way!"

CAUSE FOR FEAR

Come, little rabbit, don't be frightened of me.
It's only a habit of yours to flee
At the first sign of danger, with never a thought
Of taking precautions against getting caught.

You live in your burrow so deep underground
That only by ferrets can you be found.
At evening when rabbits should be running loose
In a field or a hedgerow, a horrible noose
Which was set by a poacher with devilish care
Might catch the unwary rabbit or hare.

Or at noontide, when rabbits are having their fun,
In the cornfield or garden, a man with a gun
May come looking for something to put in his pot;
Then rabbits should stop, and be off like a shot.

But I, little rabbit, am just hoping to get
You out of that window, and home as my pet.

ABSENCE MAKES THE HEART

If you go down on the farm one day
Be sure to use your eyes.
Take care in where you're walking -
A farm is where danger lies.
It's not an adventure playground
For children to run and hide,
And many who thought it was just that
Have been hurt, or maimed, or died.

The tractor is more than a great big toy
In the hands of a child untaught.
It's a killer which claims a girl or boy
Without giving a second thought.
So avoid these machines of the farmer -
The harvester, baler and plough;
There's many a child who would give an arm
To be able to be with us now.
But there's many a child too who DID give an arm
Or a hand or a leg or an eye,
And many a parent who should have warned
And with whom some blame must lie.

Take heed then, and please be careful
For down on the farm danger's rife.
Enjoy what you see.......but don't forget me,
For an accident ended **my** life.

LITTLE HELPERS
(Dedicated to my own children)

Hello Daddy, can I help you?
Yes my son, pass me that fork.
We are going to dig the garden
So more of 'dig' and less of 'talk'.
Here's a weed. No, it's a flower.
Can I pull it up? **You dare!**
That is one of my geraniums.
Leave it! Oh, he's stripped it bare.

Do you HAVE to come and help me?
Daddy, look, I've found a worm.
*Nice and fat….***NO, you can't eat it.**
Stand there where the ground is firm.
Now what have you got? Don't touch it-
That's a toadstool in the grass.
Are these fairies in our garden?
No, just bits of broken glass.
Leave them be, they'll cut your fingers.
S'pose I'd better clear them up.
Can I please get down to gardening?
Oh, here's Mummy with a cup.

There, that's better. "Thank you, Mummy",
Jonathan wants to go indoors.
Sweet relief, but – now what's happening?
Never rains but what it pours.
*Hello, Daddy, **I** shall help you.*
Thank you, Bethan, you are sweet.
You can help me pick some flowers
Watch out where you put your feet!

Cabbages and cauliflowers
All are flattened at a stroke
By my happy little daughter –
Seems to think it's all a joke.
Bye-bye, Daddy, I shall go now,
I did help you. Oh, you did.
MORAL – if you own a garden
Don't expect help from your kid.

PRETEND

I don't like to climb those stairs
When Dad says "Time for bed".
And so, to stall, I pretend my bears
Are waiting to be fed.
I hesitate, procrastinate,
Until my Mum sees red,
And then I'm off to say my prayers
But, when they're safely said
I pretend I'm down a coal mine
And cover up my head.
Or conquering jungle islands
From which savages have fled.
I sail across the seven seas –
Well, the Channel and the Med
Are really all I've learned about
From what my teacher said.
I walk the scorching deserts
Where only camels tread,
And here and there see skeletons
From which the blood has bled.
Sometimes I am a milkman
With a peaked cap on my head,
Or bake a bakers dozen
Of my favourite crusty bread.

But when morning comes, and Mummy cries
"Come on then, sleepyhead"
Then that's the time, as sure as eggs,
I'd rather be in bed.

To donate to the Pancreatic Cancer Research Fund charity please refer to www.pcrf.org.uk or tel. 020 8360 1119.

ACKNOWLEDGMENTS

The photographs used for the following poems are by Grey Wolf, and are used with permission: The Road To Destiny, The Turning of The Worm, This Sound of Love, Vietnam Remembered, The Thief, Centre of My Universe, and Absence Makes The Heart.

The photograph used for Unknown Destiny is an original by Derek Roberts, from the collection of Grey Wolf, and was used to illustrate the novel 'Never The Dawn'.

The photograph for Little Helpers is an original by Sandra Sztuba, from the collection of Grey Wolf.

All other photographs are by the author.

Formatting and arrangement by The Wolfian Press
www.facebook.com/thewolfianpress